THE RHYME OF THE FLYING BOMB

THE RHYME OF THE
FLYING BOMB

MERVYN PEAKE

With 22 illustrations by the Author

COLIN SMYTHE LIMITED
GERRARDS CROSS
1973

This edition published in 1973 by
Colin Smythe Ltd., Gerrards Cross,
Buckinghamshire.

SBN 900675 934

PRINTED IN GREAT BRITAIN BY OFFSET LITHOGRAPHY BY
BILLING AND SONS LTD., GUILDFORD AND LONDON

A babe was born in the reign of George
To a singular birth-bed song,
Its boisterous tune was off the beat
And all of its words were wrong;

But a singular song it was, for the house
As it rattled its ribs and danced,
Had a chorus of doors that slammed their jaws
And a chorus of chairs that pranced.

I

And the thud of the double-bass was shot
With the wail of the floating strings,
And the murderous notes of the ice-bright glass
Set sail with a clink of wings—

Set sail from the bursted window-frame
To stick in the wall like spears,
Or to slice off the heads of the birthday flowers
Or to nest on a chest-of-drawers.

And a hurdling siren wailed with love
And the windows bulged with red,
And the babe that was born in the reign of George
Wailed back from its raddled bed.

And its mother died when the roof ran in
And over the counterpane,
And the babe that was born in the reign of George
Was found in a golden drain

Was found in a fire-bright drain asleep
By a sailor dazed and lost
In a waterless world where the searchlights climbed
The sky with their fingers crossed.

Through streets where the little red monkey flames
Run over the roofs and hop
From beam to beam, and hang by their tails
Or pounce on a table-top—

Through streets where the monkey-flames run wild
And slide down the banisters.
The sailor strode with the new-born babe
To the hiss of the falling stars.

Through streets where over the window-sills
The loose wallpapers pour
And ripple their waters of nursery whales
By the light of a world at war;

And ripple their wastes of bulls and bears
And their meadows of corn and hay
In a harvest of love that was cut off short
By the scythe of an ape at play—

Through the scarlet streets and the yellow lanes
And the houses like shells of gold
With never a sign of a living soul
The sailor carried the child.

And a ton came down on a coloured road,
And a ton came down on a gaol,
And a ton came down on a freckled girl,
And a ton on the black canal,

And a ton came down on a hospital,
And a ton on a manuscript,
And a ton shot up through the dome of a church,
And a ton roared down to the crypt.

And a ton danced over the Thames and filled
A thousand panes with stars,
And the splinters leapt on the Surrey shore
To the tune of a thousand scars.

And the babe that was born in the reign of George
Lay asleep in the sailor's arm,
With the bombs for its birthday lullaby
And the flames for its birthday dream.

The sailor looked down at the doll in the crook
Of his arm with a salty sigh,
It was naked and red as a rose in the light
Of a last low evening ray.

And he lifted the wrinkled doll in his hand
Like a watch to his frost-bit ear,
And he heard the tick of its heart beat quick
On the drum as he held it there.

"What kind of a lark is this?" he said
"And what'll I do? To hell
With finding a babe in a golden drain
With its ticker at work'n all.

I would rather my god,damn sea of salt
That is master of bomb an' fire
Though it stung my heart when it drowned my mate
In the thick of its midnight hair.

I would rather the sea that can sting the heart
In a way I can understand
Than this London raw as an open sore
And a new,born babe in my hand."

The sailor trod over the glittering glass
A,dazzle with jags of red
And came to a man leaning over a wall
With his shadow above his head.

"Can you tell me the nearest First Aid Post"
The sailor said to the man,
But the lounging figure made no reply
For the back of his head was gone.

The sailor wiped the sweat from his face
And he laughed in a hapless way,
"O Christ! little fish" he said to the babe
"This isn't no place to stay.

This isn't no place for the likes of you
Nor it is for the likes of me
We'd be better asleep in a hammock, we would,
On the wet of the mine-filled sea.

We'd be far better off where the soldiers are
Than naked in London town
Where a house can rock like a rocking-horse
And the bright bricks tumble down.

All bare and cold in that gutter of gold
You had no cause to be,
No more than it's right for the likes of you
To be born in this century.

But the sky is bright though it's late at night
And the colours are gay as gay
And the glass that is lodged in my hip bone now
Is jabbing from far away.

And the warding off of that burning beam
Has hurt my shoulder sore,
And I want to laugh! O my little blind fish!
And dance on the golden floor.

See! See! Ha! Ha! how the dazzling streets
Are empty from end to end
With only a cat with a splinter through its heart,
And an arm where the railings end."

And the sailor threw back his head and laughed
In a way that was loud and torn,
And even his mother would never have guessed
That his face was the face of her son.

And over his mind like a flutter of leaves
His scare-crow memories fell
And the light in his eye was the wrecker's light
That burns on the wharves of hell.

And his dance was a scare-crow dance, and his feet
Clashed loud on the streets of glass,
And his bones shone red and were sticky with his blood
While he signed for the ships to pass.

And the ships of brick and the ships of stone
And the charcoal ships lurched by
While his footsteps clashed on the frozen waves
That shone to the scarlet sky.

While raised aloft and for'ard of his heart
Like a small, bright figurehead,
Lay the babe in the crib of his bowsprit arm,
Asleep like a babe in bed.

Like a babe in the cot of a golden storm
It opened its new-born eye
To the shuffle of the warm, red, restless air
And the dazzle of the witchcraft sky.

"Watch me! watch me!" cried the man from the sea
With his long and scare-crow legs,
As he leapt like a spider on the foreign shore
Of a million coral-jags.

And he pranced like a spider through the fire-torn door
Of a church where a headless horse
Lay stiff in the smouldering aisle with a hoof
At its heart like the sign of the cross.

And he leapt the horse with a mantis leap,
And he came to the front row pew
And he laid the babe on the charcoal bench
And he turned to where the pulpit grew.

It grew from a mound of tapers and stones
And bibles and deep blue glass,
But its carven top had been left by the bomb
Exactly as it always was.

But the steps were gone and he swarmed the side
Like a pilot and came aboard
And stood for a moment with his heavy hands
On the gull-winged word of God.

And there, below, like a spark of light
In the deep of the church was the babe
With its new-born eyes wide open on his own
And its hands on the charcoal slab.

And lo, from the bedlam sky had flown
The last black bomber away
And the air was quiet in the crag-walled church
And the dawn was an hour away.

"O my little bright fish!" the sailor cried
In a voice as gruff as a gun,
"Shall I worship you now from this crows-nest here
In the silence what's just begun?

Shall I worship you now for your brand-new look
And your brand-new arms and legs
And your fists like a brace of anemones,
And your body as soft as an egg?

O, Christ in heaven! I must worship you
For the ticker you keep in your chest;
I must worship you for your new-look, babe,
That'll never be washed or dressed.

With the light of your eyes so fixed on mine
Then strong as a lion I am!
The lion of Judah, or Africa
Or the one that lay down with the lamb.

O watch me quick! for my mane burns thick
With its locks of yellow and black!
The world that lopes through the night above
Can never come loping back."

The sailor jumped with a single jump
And stood on the pulpit's rim,
"Now listen to me while I sing you a tale
To the tune of a bleeding hymn!

For the things I've forgotten for many a year
Are shouldering into my mind
Of a time when my heart was a wave that heaved
To the gale of my sea-mad mind."

He spread out his hands like a starfish brown
At the sides of his big rough head;
"Will you listen to me, my finless fish
As you lie on your wrinkled bed?"

"I will! I will!" came a cry as shrill
And thin as river-reed,
"I am wide awake and the church is still,
O sailor I will indeed.

"I will! I will!" cried the new-born babe,
"Though I've lived it all before
For there's nothing new when the womb is through
With its restless prisoner."

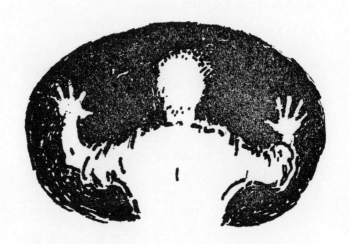

And the babe sprang up on the charcoal pew
And stretched out its wrinkled arms,
O, a sprite it was, or a gull or a frog
Or a grape or a bud as it blooms.

"O listen my sailor, saviour man,
Though the world is a place that's wide,
There's nothing outside of the womb of Eve
That you wouldn't have known inside.

If you tell me a tale I shall listen well
To the roll of your salt-sea voice—
But I'd rather be singing along with you
As we sang in the early days.

For, sailor, there's nothing that is not true
If it's true to your heart and mine
From a unicorn to a flying bomb
From a wound to a glass of wine."

"O my new-born sprite with your eyes alight
Be careful as you call!
I wouldn't have you crash upon the cold, stone floor
With your limbs so soft and small."

The new-born babe soared up in the air
To the head of a candlestick
Where it hovered with its hands clenched tight at its
    breast
At the height of the gull-winged Book.

"I have swarmed the masts of a thousand fleets,
I have drowned through the bruise-blue sea,
I have burned through an age of scarlet fires
So have no fear of me."

"Ahoy then! my cockleshell babe aloft
On your candlestick mast so high!
What a time we'd have had all over the world
On the waters of yesterday!"

"I remember well!" cried the hovering babe,
"I remember everything;
You have only to sing, my war-time friend
And I will know what to sing."

Then the sailor lifted his deep-sea voice,
And the naked babe cried shrill
Of a day that had been in the sailor's blood
For as long as his heart could tell—

Of a day that was far away in his blood
But as close as breath to the babe
And as vivid to each as the fires that night
Or the blood of the London curb.

And the song flew on like a hundred songs
That grow in the brain like grass
"It was long ago, it was long ago
Or ever the world war was."

"It was long ago" cried the voice of the babe,
"Far further than yesterday"
And the sailor cried, "It was long ago
And a million miles away."

And as they sang a cold light ran
From the east of London town
And shone upon the horse with its hoof at its heart
And the hymn books crisp and brown.

"O sailor, saviour, the dawn is up!
And the fires are dying down;
What a lovely light for my birthday bright
With the birds of iron flown."

But the scare-crow sailor made no reply,
For his limbs shook suddenly
And the golden fume that had filled his brain
Slid cruelly away.

Then the babe, with a leap was at his side
And had knelt on the Holy Word—
"I am frightened, little fish, O what can it be
That my heart beats high and hard!

And my strength is ebbing away from me
And the lion in my breast has died,
O what can it be that from head to foot
I am now so terrified?"

"Step down from the pulpit's walnut rim"
Said the voice of the infant child
"And join your hands by the side of the word
While the light of the dawn is spilled;

For your brain is alone now your passion goes,
And your coloured dreams run cold
And there's nothing left but a gaping skull
On the spine of the wounded world.

But we are well! O sailor! sailor!
O we are very well!
Do not tremble as you stand, O frightened sailor
For death is so mean and small.

It snatches away the burning breath
And it snatches at the useless clay
But what can it do to halt the square-rigged
Soul as it steers away?"

"What use is my soul" cried the trembling sailor,
"When my breath is torn away?
O naked babe who can speak like a man
Have you nothing but that to say?"

"O sailor, saviour, you rescued me
And I would not have you cry
If you have no Faith yet your act was Love
The greatest of the three.

And out of your love, O frightened sailor
You showed me the coloured lights,
And the golden shoals of the falling stones,
And the scarlet of the streets;

And I am rich on my natal day
With such rare tragedy
That I have no fear, but only long
That you could be rich like me.

And I who have died a thousand times
Will cheer you as you die—
O hark! how the sirens wail to us
From Dover by the sea.

Let us lure them here, the returning raiders—
O let us lure them here!
That we may explode in one flash of love
At the height of a world at war.

For the steed of God has died in the aisle
And the stained glass glowers blue,
I have lived so deep in this natal day
That there is no more to know."

But the sailor cried "O child, if it's true
That you've lived all this before,
What kind of comfort is that to me
Who can never come back for more?

I am no magical thing like you
And half of my life has gone;
You can speak like a man, and perch in the air,
Though you've only been four hours born,

But I am not ready to die, O child
I am not ready to die
Dear Christ, If my hands and my eyes were gone
I would not be ready to die."

Down the burning cheek of the naked babe
A tear slid heavily
As though it were taking the curve of the world—
And then, as the stillness lay

Like a throbbing weight, the low sun shone
On the ruins that hemmed them in,
The babe who was born in the reign of George
Knelt down on the pulpit's rim.

"What instrument can measure the Grace
Of God?" the new-born said
"Or prove the truth of your earthless soul
Until your body is dead.

There is no proof that the flames to-night
So tall and so luminous
Were as rare as the colours of Zion are
Where the flocks of Jesus graze—

Nor is there proof that you rescued me
Because of the love of God.
O sailor, sailor, there is no proof
Until your body is dead."

"But my body is what has laughed for me!
And my body is what has cried!
Where are the tears of my spirit, child?
And how are its cheekbones dried?

These hands of mine I can understand
Far more than a ransomed soul,
This mouth has crushed the reddest lips
That ever blazed on a girl. . . ."

But as he spoke the wailing broke
Out louder and more loud,
From town to town the banshee cried
Out of the morning cloud.

From town to town the sirens passed
The news of death's approach
Until the warm air leapt like waves
Within the ruined church

And then, a sudden silence fell
Upon the house of God
And, in the silence . . . presently . . .
A ticking sound was heard.

And louder, louder, momently
Until the ticking was
The stuttering of a far machine
Intent upon its course.

And then, across the thickening air—
"Look! look! O sailor! see!
Who is it stands and wrings her hands
Beside the molten Tree?"

O terrible! Incalculable!
Christ's Mother! The long sound
Of hammers in the London sky
Beats on the open wound.

"Can you not see her? Sailor, saviour,
With the rubble at her feet?
Or hear above the flying Bomb
The huge beats of her heart?"

"My blood has filled my broken shoes
And I am too weak to see
The Virgin now or any ghost
I am so ill and dizzy. . . ."

"I am too sick to hear a heart
Beat in a phantom's body—
O tell me, little fish, how long
Before I have to die?"

"Not long, not long, the engine claws
God's face and tears His hands,
O saviour, sailor, take me down
To where his Mother stands.

She cannot see: her hands are clenched
Across her eyes, the swords
Of Love have driven her so far
Along so many roads.

Through history, from Bethlehem
Is far to walk alone
One thousand and nine years
And forty-one, are gone. . . ."

And closer sped the flying cross:
The rattling of its throat
Tossed up the air and shook the shell
Of heaven's battered fort.

The sailor held the new-born sprite,
Fresh mint of George's reign—
And swarming deckwards through the storm
His joy returned again—

His joy returned—his brain broke loose,
And scampered far away
"Now God be praised," he yelled "the ships
Of hell are in the bay!

A hundred thousand fire-green crows
Are perched upon the spars
And croak at me 'O sailor see
The brilliance of our claws.

We are the long lost tribe of all
That you've been waiting for!'
How glorious it is to sway
Upon the waves of war!

The masts are bright with silver light
The decks are black with grass
And the bay's so smooth that I can see
The blood beneath the glass.

And here's a child, and there's a child
Running across the bay
They laugh and shout 'Look out! look out!
We haven't long to stay!'

And here's a man who somersaults
Across the mid-mast air
The long-shore flames leap out to sea
And drag him by the hair.

And the guns that shine with oil and wine
Are smothered in sea-flowers deep,
And in the throat of every gun
A mermaid lies asleep.

And the figurehead with mouth so red
Is drinking up the sea. . . .
O little babe, why won't you leap
Aboard, and sail with me?"

"I will," the new-born babe replied
"O sailor I will, and more—
But hark! the *silence* of the cross
That we've been waiting for."

A long black wall like a rotting sail
Stood waving to and fro
It was as though the heavy air
Pressed upwards from below.

It waved and waved and could not fall
Through such portentous air,
While silence like a ghost let down
The long ice of its hair.

When the dead horse rose on its armoured feet
And strode to where they stood,
The crash of its hooves on the hollow stones
Was like the gongs of God.

And the babe slid out of the sailor's coat
And hovered above his head,
And the blood of the babe was mixed with the oozing
Flow of the sailor's blood.

When the silence broke and the air was filled
With the whirr of the diving cross
While the babe hung poised and the fainting sailor
Leaned on the headless horse.

And the church leapt out of a lake of light
And the pews were rows of fire,
And the golden cock crowed thrice and flew
From the peak of the falling spire.

And the candlewax swam over the stones,
And the tail of the flying Bomb
Stuck out of the floor to point the place
That it had journeyed from.

While plunged below in the shattered crypt
Was the skull of the scalding head,
And the short black wings that made the cross
Were splashed with the sailor's blood.

And the dust rose up from the hills of brick
And hung over London town,
And a thousand roofs grew soft and thick
With the dust as it settled down.

And the morning light shone clear and bright
On a city as gold as grain,
While the babe that was born in the reign of George
Lay coiled in the womb again.